Cambridge Key English Test 1

Examination papers from the University of Cambridge Local Examinations Syndicate

PUBLISHED BY THE PRESS SYNDICATE OF THE UNIVERSITY OF CAMBRIDGE
The Pitt Building, Trumpington Street, Cambridge CB2 1RP, United Kingdom

CAMBRIDGE UNIVERSITY PRESS
The Edinburgh Building, Cambridge CB2 2RU, United Kingdom
40 West 20th Street, New York, NY 1011-4211, USA
10 Stamford Road, Oakleigh, Melbourne 3166, Australia

© Cambridge University Press 1997

This book is in copyright. Subject to statutory exception
and to the provisions of relevant collective licensing agreements,
no reproduction of any part may take place without
the written permission of Cambridge University Press.

First published 1997
Reprinted 1998

Printed in the United Kingdom at the University Press, Cambridge

ISBN 0 521 58729 8   Student's Book
ISBN 0 521 58728 X   Teacher's Book
ISBN 0 521 58727 1   Cassette

Contents

To the student iv

Test 1 Paper 1 1
Paper 2 13
Paper 3 20

Test 2 Paper 1 21
Paper 2 33
Paper 3 40

Test 3 Paper 1 41
Paper 2 53
Paper 3 60

Test 4 Paper 1 61
Paper 2 73
Paper 3 80

Visual materials for Paper 3 81

Sample answer sheets 90

Acknowledgements *inside back cover*

To the student

This book is for students preparing for the University of Cambridge Local Examinations Syndicate (UCLES) Key English Test (KET). It contains four complete tests based on past papers from April 1995 to March 1996.

What is KET?

KET is an examination for students of English as a foreign language. It tests Reading, Writing, Listening and Speaking. The KET examination is at Cambridge Level One.

Paper 1	1 hour 10 minutes	**Reading and Writing**	8 parts	50% of total marks
Paper 2	about 25 minutes	**Listening**	5 parts	25% of total marks
Paper 3	8–10 minutes	**Speaking**	2 parts	25% of total marks

How do I prepare for KET?

It is important to know what type of questions are in the KET examination. Doing the tests in this book will help you. Practise putting your answers on the sample answer sheets on pages 90 to 92 (you may photocopy these pages). This will help you to understand what you have to do in the real test.

Reading: Read some books in simple English from your library or local bookshop. Try to guess the words you don't know before you use a dictionary to check them. Also, use an English learner's dictionary when you study. If you live in a tourist area, there may be some signs or notices in English outside restaurants and shops or in railway stations and airports. Read these and try to understand them.

Writing: Write short letters or messages in English to a friend who is learning English with you or find an English-speaking pen friend to write to. Write about your daily life (your home, work or school and your family). If you go on holiday, write postcards in English and send them to your English-speaking friends.

Listening: Listen to the cassettes that come with English course books so you can hear different people speaking English. Watch English-language programmes on television and listen to English on the radio if possible.

Speaking: Talk in English with friends who are studying with you. Ask each other questions about your daily lives, your future plans and about other towns, countries or places you have visited.

We hope this book helps you when you take the KET examination. Good luck!

Test 1

PAPER 1 READING AND WRITING (1 hour 10 minutes)

PART 1
QUESTIONS 1 – 5

Where can you see these notices?
For questions 1 – 5, mark A, B or C on the answer sheet.

EXAMPLE		ANSWER
0 *Return books here*	A in a restaurant B in a bank C in a library	C

1 Today's weather inside on page 6
    A in a book
    B on television
    C in a newspaper

2 2ND FLOOR *Children's Clothes*
    A on a shirt
    B in a shop
    C in a school

3 PARKING FOR CUSTOMERS ONLY
    A outside a restaurant
    B outside a school
    C outside a hospital

4 MORE TABLES UPSTAIRS
    A in a theatre
    B at a camping-site
    C in a café

5 BEST BEFORE December '98
    A on clothes
    B on machines
    C on food

QUESTIONS 6 – 10

Which notice (A – H) says this (6 – 10)?
For questions 6 – 10, mark the correct letter A – H on the answer sheet.

EXAMPLE	ANSWER
0 We can answer your questions.	E

6   You can't drive this way.

7   Children do not have to pay.

8   You can shop here six days a week.

9   Be careful when you stand up.

10   We work quickly.

A   *Adults £2.50 Under 12s FREE*

B   Shoes repaired while you wait

C   MIND YOUR HEAD

D   Open 24 hours a day

E   INFORMATION

F   Police Notice Road Closed

G   Open daily 10–6 (except Mondays)

H   WAITING ROOM

PART 2

QUESTIONS 11 – 15

Read the sentences (11 – 15) about holidays and travel.
What is the correct word (A – H) for each sentence?
For questions 11 – 15, mark the correct letter A – H on the answer sheet.

EXAMPLE	ANSWER
0 You write on this and send it to your friends.	D

11   This person gives you holiday information.

12   You need to buy one before you get on a plane.

13   This is where you go to get a plane.

14   You put your clothes in this when you travel.

15   This person likes visiting different places.

A airport

B camera

C passport

D postcard

E suitcase

F ticket

G tourist

H travel agent

PART 3

QUESTIONS 16 – 20

Complete the five conversations.
For conversations 16 – 20, mark A, B or C on the answer sheet.

16 It's time for lunch.

A Oh good!
B One hour.
C Half-past twelve.

17 Would you like a drink?

A I don't like coffee.
B I prefer tea.
C Coffee, please.

18 How much was your new shirt?

A It's a red shirt.
B It was very cheap.
C It was in a shop.

19 I'm very sorry.

A I'm afraid so.
B I think so.
C That's all right.

20 Do you speak English?

A No, I'm not.
B Only a little.
C Yes, very much.

QUESTIONS 21 – 25

Complete this conversation at a garage.
What does the woman say to the car mechanic?
For questions 21 – 25, mark the correct letter A – H on the answer sheet.

EXAMPLE	ANSWER
Mechanic: Good morning, Madam. What's the problem?	
Woman: **0**	B

Mechanic: What do you mean?

Woman: **21** ....

Mechanic: I see. We can probably repair that easily. Can you leave the car now?

Woman: **22** ....

Mechanic: I'm sorry. We're completely full on Saturday.

Woman: **23** ....

Mechanic: Yes, all right. Could you come in the morning?

Woman: **24** ....

Mechanic: OK.

Woman: **25** ....

Mechanic: I'm not sure, but probably about £30.

Woman: That's fine. I'll see you on Monday.

A I'd prefer the afternoon.

B I'm not sure. The brakes aren't working very well.

C Oh! One other thing, how much will it cost?

D The engine is hard to start in the morning.

E I work on Mondays.

F I'm afraid I need it today. How about the weekend?

G When I brake, the car goes to the left.

H Oh. Could you do it on Monday?

Test 1

PART 4

QUESTIONS 26 – 32

Read the information about three books and then answer the questions.
For questions 26 – 32, mark A, B or C on the answer sheet.

New books this month

The Long Night
This is David Reilly's first book. David became a writer after teaching English for several years.
Maha is a nurse in northern Australia, where she works in a small hospital. One day a baby is so ill that Maha has to drive all night to get her to the nearest big city. They have a lot of problems getting there and …

Hard Work
This exciting story is Joanna Jones's twentieth.
'Hard Work' is about Sombat, who works with his father, a carpenter, in Thailand. They work long, hard hours making tables and chairs, but they do not have any money. Then one day a man dressed all in black buys the most beautiful table in the shop …

Hospital or Cinema?
Marcie Jacome, who studies English in London, wrote this story earlier this year.
Tina is a young Brazilian woman whose dream is to become a doctor. She goes to London to study English and medicine but one day she meets a man who asks her to go to the USA with him to become a film star … What will Tina do?

6

Paper 1: Reading and Writing

EXAMPLE			ANSWER
0 Which book is about somebody who works with doctors?			A
A The Long Night	**B** Hard Work	**C** Hospital or Cinema?	

26 Which book is by somebody who has written a lot of books?

    A The Long Night   **B** Hard Work   **C** Hospital or Cinema?

27 Which book is about somebody who is very poor?

    A The Long Night   **B** Hard Work   **C** Hospital or Cinema?

28 Which book is about somebody who would like to work in a hospital?

    A The Long Night   **B** Hard Work   **C** Hospital or Cinema?

29 Which book is by somebody who worked in a school?

    A The Long Night   **B** Hard Work   **C** Hospital or Cinema?

30 Which book is about a difficult journey?

    A The Long Night   **B** Hard Work   **C** Hospital or Cinema?

31 Which book is about a man and his son?

    A The Long Night   **B** Hard Work   **C** Hospital or Cinema?

32 Which book is by a student?

    A The Long Night   **B** Hard Work   **C** Hospital or Cinema?

PART 5

QUESTIONS 33 – 40

Read the information about Schnauzer dogs.
Choose the best word (A, B or C) for each space (33 – 40).
For questions 33 – 40, mark A, B or C on the answer sheet.

Schnauzer Dogs

There are three sizes **0** Schnauzer dog.

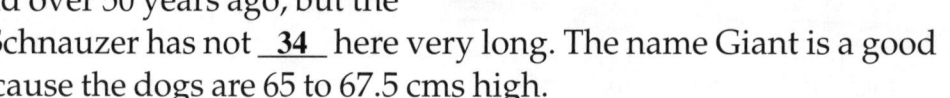

The two smaller sizes first **33** to England over 50 years ago, but the Giant Schnauzer has not **34** here very long. The name Giant is a good one because the dogs are 65 to 67.5 cms high.

All the dogs **35** long hair, which should be cut quite often. Most smaller Schnauzers **36** grey in colour, **37** the Giant Schnauzer is usually black.

Schnauzers come from Germany, where farmers use the dogs to help **38** with their sheep, and they are also used **39** the police, because Schnauzer dogs are very intelligent.

A Schnauzer makes **40** nice family dog. It is friendly and very good with young children.

EXAMPLE						ANSWER
0	A with	B of		C in		B

33 A came   B come   C comes
34 A being   B be   C been
35 A has   B have   C had
36 A were   B is   C are
37 A or   B if   C but
38 A them   B him   C us
39 A from   B by   C to
40 A the   B a   C any

9

PART 6

QUESTIONS 41 – 50

Complete this letter.
Write ONE word for each space (41 – 50).
For questions 41 – 50, write your words on the answer sheet.

---

28 Long Road
Brighton

22nd March

Dear Pat,

I arrived (*Example:* here) three weeks ago. I'm studying at a language school __41__ Brighton. The students come __42__ many different countries and I __43__ made a lot of new friends.

There __44__ classes for five hours every day. I like __45__ teacher very much. __46__ name is John and he helps me __47__ I make a mistake.

I want __48__ visit London next weekend because I __49__ going back to my country on Monday. Can I see you there? Please write to __50__ soon.

With best wishes from

Maria

Paper 1: Reading and Writing

PART 7

QUESTIONS 51 – 55

Read this note from Sheila.
Fill in the information about the Film Club.
For questions 51 – 55, write the information on the answer sheet.

Andy,

About the next Film Club evening – it's going to be in October, on the 15th (which is a Tuesday). The film will be 'The Last Emperor' and tickets will cost £3.00. We can have Room 26 from 8 o'clock.

Thanks.
         Sheila

COLLEGE FILM CLUB

NEXT MEETING

DAY:		*Tuesday*
DATE:	51	
TIME:	52	
PLACE:	53	
FILM:	54	
PRICE:	55	

Test 1

PART 8
QUESTION 56

Read the note from your friend Richard.
Write a postcard to tell him what he wants to know.

> It's great that you're coming to see me in England. Tell me when you are coming, how long you want to stay and what you want to do.
>
> Write soon!
>
> Richard

Write 20 – 25 words.
Write your answer on the answer sheet.

PAPER 2 LISTENING (approximately 25 minutes)

PART 1
QUESTIONS 1 – 5

Listen to the tape.
You will hear five short conversations.
You will hear each conversation twice.
There is one question for each conversation.
For questions 1 – 5, put a tick ☑ under the right answer.

EXAMPLE

0   What time is it?

06.00	08.00	09.00
A ☐	B ☐	C ☑

---

1   What have they forgotten?

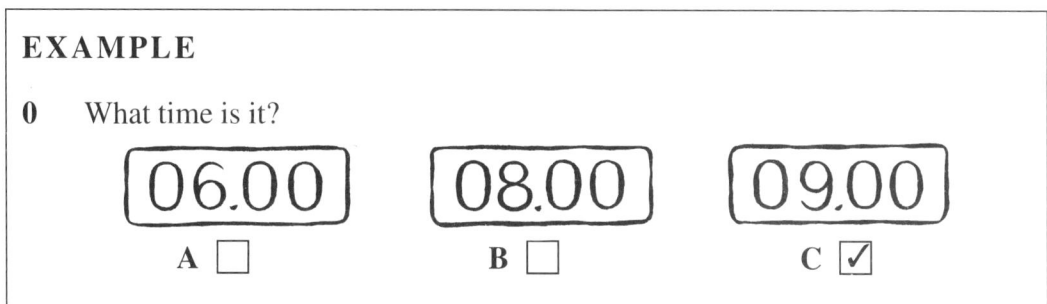

A ☐   B ☐   C ☐

2   What time does the train go?

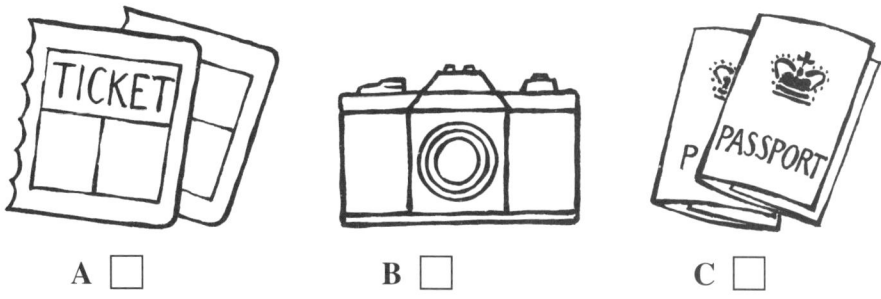

A ☐   B ☐   C ☐

Test 1

3 Where is Room 22?

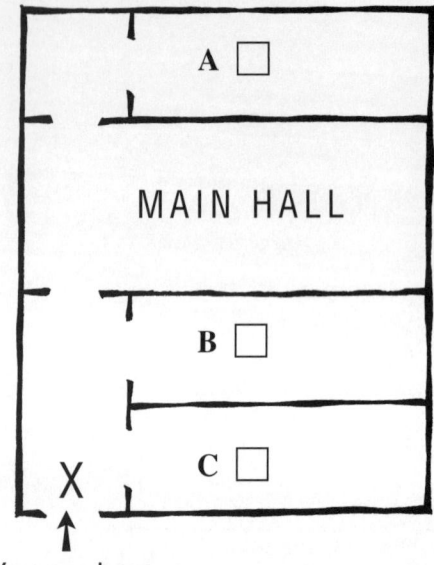

4 Which man wants to see him?

5 How did the woman get to work?

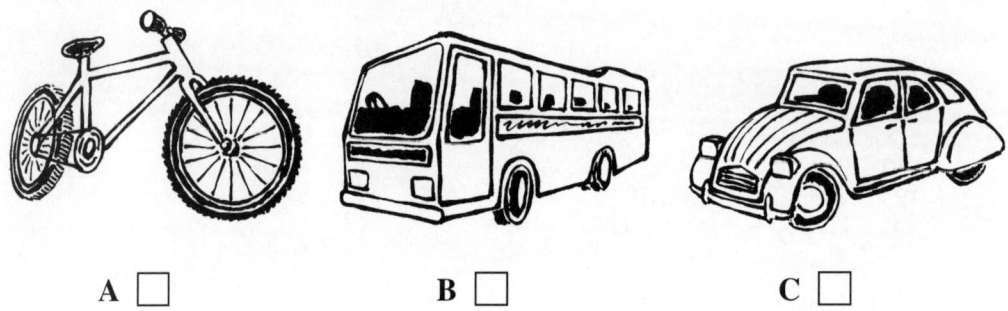

Paper 2: Listening

PART 2

QUESTIONS 6 – 10

Listen to Paul talking to a friend about his family.
What does each person do?

For questions 6 – 10, write a letter A – H next to each person.
You will hear the conversation twice.

EXAMPLE		
0	Sally	H

PEOPLE

6   Bill   ☐

7   David   ☐

8   Paul's mother ☐

9   Paul's father ☐

10 Paul   ☐

JOBS

A   bank clerk

B   doctor

C   farmer

D   shop assistant

E   stopped work

F   student

G   teacher

H   writer

15

Test 1

PART 3

QUESTIONS 11 – 15

Eric and Mary are talking about the weekend.
Their friend, Carlos, is coming to visit them.

For questions 11 – 15, tick ✓ A, B or C.
You will hear the conversation twice.

EXAMPLE

0   What does Carlos hate?

   A   shopping   ✓

   B   museums   ☐

   C   football   ☐

---

11   When is the football match?

   A   Saturday morning   ☐

   B   Saturday afternoon   ☐

   C   Sunday afternoon   ☐

12   Where are they going to eat on Saturday evening?

   A   at home   ☐

   B   in an Italian restaurant ☐

   C   in a Chinese restaurant   ☐

13   What are they going to do on Sunday morning?

   A   go for a drive   ☐

   B   get up late   ☐

   C   go to the cinema   ☐

Paper 2: Listening

14 Where are they going to have lunch on Sunday?

    A   in a café ☐

    B   in a pub ☐

    C   at home ☐

15 They can't go to the cinema on Sunday afternoon because

    A   Carlos doesn't like films. ☐

    B   Eric doesn't like films. ☐

    C   they don't have time. ☐

Test 1

PART 4

QUESTIONS 16 – 20

Listen to a telephone conversation.
A girl wants to speak to Martin, but he is not there.

For questions 16 – 20, complete the message to Martin.
You will hear the conversation twice.

Phone Message

To: *Martin*

From: **16** _____

Party at: **17** _____

Time: **18** _____

Please bring: **19** _____

Her phone number: **20** _____

Paper 2: Listening

PART 5

QUESTIONS 21 – 25

Listen to some information about a travel agency.

Listen and complete questions 21 – 25.
You will hear the information twice.

South Seas Travel Agency

New phone number:	847 2296
New address:	21 98 .... Road
Opposite:	22
Opens on:	23
Book a holiday for:	24 £
and get a free:	25

You now have 8 minutes to write your answers on the answer sheet.

Test 1

PAPER 3   SPEAKING

The Speaking test lasts 8 to 10 minutes. You will take the test with another candidate. There are two examiners, but only one of them will talk to you. The examiner will ask you questions and ask you to talk to the other candidate.

Part 1 (5 – 6 minutes)

The examiner will ask you and your partner some questions. These questions will be about your daily life, past experience and future plans. For example, you may have to speak about your school, job, hobbies or home town.

Part 2 (3 – 4 minutes)

You and your partner will speak to each other. You will ask and answer questions.

Either:

The examiner will give you a card with some words and pictures on it. You will ask your partner five questions using this card. Your partner will answer the questions. Then you will change roles.

Or:

The examiner will give you a card with some information on it. The examiner will give your partner a card with some words on it. Your partner will use the words on the card to ask you questions about the information you have. Then you will change roles.

Test 2

PAPER 1   READING AND WRITING (1 hour 10 minutes)

PART 1
QUESTIONS 1 – 5

Where can you see these notices?
For questions 1 – 5, mark A, B or C on the answer sheet.

EXAMPLE   **ANSWER**

0   *Return books here*
    A   in a restaurant
    B   in a bank   C
    C   in a library

---

1   **NO** Food in Classrooms
    A   in a restaurant
    B   in a hotel
    C   in a school

2   *Pull*
    A   on a menu
    B   on a road
    C   on a door

3   Please put your postage stamp here.
    A   on an envelope
    B   in a book
    C   in a newspaper

4   *Stairs to first floor*
    A   in a shop
    B   in a taxi
    C   in a park

5   DANGER Low Bridge
    A   in a hospital
    B   on a road
    C   in a lift

QUESTIONS 6 – 10

Which notice (A – H) says this (6 – 10)?
For questions 6 – 10, mark the correct letter A – H on the answer sheet.

EXAMPLE	ANSWER
0 You can leave your suitcase here.	C

6   You must drive carefully here.

7   You can eat cheaply here.

8   You can stay here on holiday.

9   You can find work here.

10   You must not go in this way.

A   NO SERVICE STATION ON MOTORWAY

B   *Travel Express* NEW BUSINESS HOURS 9 A.M–6 P.M.

C   LEFT LUGGAGE OPEN 24 HOURS

D   PLEASE USE OTHER DOOR

E   Camp-site Open All Year

F   JOB AGENCY *We've got the right job for you!*

G   Joe's Snack Bar Lowest Prices in Town!

H   DANGER! ICE ON ROAD

PART 2

QUESTIONS 11 – 15

Read the descriptions (11 – 15) of some places.
What is the name of each place (A – H)?
For questions 11 – 15, mark the correct letter A – H on the answer sheet.

EXAMPLE	ANSWER
0 You can take the train from here.	G

PLACES

11 Your car can be repaired here.

A bridge

B church

12 You go here to see a play.

C factory

D garage

13 You can watch sports here.

E hospital

14 You stay here when you are ill.

F stadium

G station

15 You can cross a river here.

H theatre

23

Test 2

PART 3

QUESTIONS 16 – 20

Complete the five conversations.
For questions 16 – 20, mark A, B or C on the answer sheet.

16 Hello, Sue. This is my boss, Mrs Smith.
    A How old is she?
    B How much is it?
    C How do you do?

17 Tell Ben to come upstairs.
    A That's right.
    B All right.
    C Is that right?

18 Have you got a ticket?
    A At the ticket office.
    B Here it is.
    C Yes, please.

19 Let's go to Brighton tomorrow.
    A What a pity!
    B OK. Why not?
    C It doesn't matter.

20 Can I open the window, please?
    A You don't.
    B It isn't.
    C Of course.

Paper 1: Reading and Writing

QUESTIONS 21 – 25

**Complete the telephone conversation.
What does Peter say to James?
For questions 21 – 25, mark the correct letter A – H on the answer sheet.**

EXAMPLE		ANSWER
James:	Hello, 345920.	
Peter:	**0**	G

James: No, I don't think so. Why?

Peter: **21** ....

James: Where are they playing?

Peter: **22** ....

James: I'd love to come. How much are the tickets?

Peter: **23** ....

James: Will we have to leave early?

Peter: **24** ....

James: What time should we meet?

Peter: **25** ....

James: Thanks, Peter. Goodbye.

Peter: Goodbye.

A They're free. My father gave them to me.

B In London. We can go in my car.

C I'll call you again on Friday to arrange the time.

D My car's very small.

E I've got some tickets for the football – England against France.

F We can meet in the town centre.

G Hello, it's Peter. Are you busy on Saturday?

H I suppose so. There may be a lot of traffic.

25

PART 4

QUESTIONS 26 – 32

Read the article about the London Police and answer the questions.
For questions 26 – 32, mark the correct letter A, B or C on the answer sheet.

THE HISTORY OF THE LONDON POLICE

Today there are policemen everywhere, but in 1700 London had no policemen at all. A few old men used to protect the city streets at night and they were not paid very much.

About 300 years ago, London was starting to get bigger. The city was very dirty and many people were poor. There were so many thieves who stole money in the streets that people stayed in their homes as much as possible.

In 1750, Henry Fielding started to pay a group of people to stop thieves. They were like policemen and were called 'Bow Street Runners' because they worked near Bow Street.

Fifty years later, there were 120 Bow Street Runners, but London had become very big and needed more policemen. So, in 1829, the first Metropolitan (or London) Police Force was started with 3000 officers. Most of the men worked on foot, but a few rode horses. Until 1920 all the police in London were men.

Today, London police are quite well paid and for the few police officers who still ride horses, the pay is even better than for the others.

EXAMPLE			ANSWER
0	In 1700, there were	A policemen everywhere.	
		B policemen only in London.	C
		C no policemen in London.	

26 In 1700, the men who protected the streets were paid
    A a lot.
    B a little.
    C nothing.

27 300 years ago, many people
    A came to live in London.
    B wanted to leave London.
    C had big houses in London.

28 People did not leave their houses because
    A the city was not clean.
    B they had no money.
    C they were afraid.

29 The Bow Street Runners
    A stole money.
    B stopped people stealing.
    C paid people to steal.

30 In 1800, there were
    A enough policemen.
    B not enough policemen.
    C too many policemen.

31 Of the first 3000 Metropolitan policemen,
    A all of them rode horses.
    B some of them rode horses.
    C most of them rode horses.

32 Today, police officers who work with horses are paid
    A more than their colleagues.
    B the same as their colleagues.
    C half as much as their colleagues.

Test 2

PART 5

QUESTIONS 33 – 40

Read the information about dinosaurs.
Choose the best word (A, B or C) for each space (33 – 40).
For questions 33 – 40, mark A, B or C on the answer sheet.

Dinosaurs

No one has __0__ seen a dinosaur. The last dinosaur died about 60 million years ago, a long time __33__ there were any people on the earth. __34__ knows for sure why they all died.
The nearest living relatives of dinosaurs are birds.

Dinosaurs didn't all look the same. There were more __35__ 5000 kinds. Some were very small, __36__ others were giants. The largest were bigger than any other animals that ever lived __37__ land. The Brontosaurus, for example, was twenty metres long, and it __38__ plants. The Tyrannosaurus Rex was not as __39__ , but it was stronger. It had sharp teeth for eating meat. Also it could run fast __40__ it had long back legs.

EXAMPLE						ANSWER
0	A ever	B	never	C	yet	A

33	A	that	B	when	C	before
34	A	Everybody	B	People	C	Nobody
35	A	than	B	that	C	as
36	A	as	B	but	C	or
37	A	in	B	on	C	at
38	A	ate	B	eat	C	eats
39	A	bigger	B	biggest	C	big
40	A	that	B	because	C	where

Test 2

PART 6

QUESTIONS 41 – 50

Complete these letters.
Write ONE word for each space (41 – 50).
For questions 41 – 50, write your words on the answer sheet.

14 Sheffield Road
Rotherham
20 May 1997

Dear Mary,

I will (*Example: be*) in London __41__ Thursday morning. Would you like to have lunch __42__ me? Write and tell __43__ when you are free and where I __44__ meet you.

Hope to see you then.

Yours

Joan

20 DIDSBURY DRIVE   LONDON NW1

25 May 1997

Dear Joan,

Thanks __45__ your letter. I got it this morning. Yes, I'd __46__ to see you. How about meeting outside __47__ office at one o'clock? There's __48__ good Italian restaurant near there. __49__ you like Italian food?

I have to be back at work by two o'clock, so please don't __50__ late!

Yours

Mary

30

PART 7

QUESTIONS 51 – 55

Read the memo to Mrs Jones.
Fill in the information on the Business Travel Form.
For questions 51 – 55, write the information on the answer sheet.

MEMO	
To:	Mrs Jones
From:	Cathy
Date:	20th August

Here is the new information for your trip to Hong Kong. You will fly from Manchester on 3rd September (not the 4th) You come back to the U.K. on 8th September. A taxi will be waiting for you at the airport (the company car is not free).

EASTWOODS CLOTHES COMPANY
Business Travel Form

Name: Mrs Jones

Place of visit: **51** _____

U.K. airport: **52** _____

Dates of travel

Leave: **53** _____

Return: **54** _____

Transport from airport: **55** _____

PART 8

QUESTION 56

Read the note from your friend Leslie.
Write to Leslie and answer his questions.

> I'm having a party at my house on Saturday.
> Can you come?
> Would you like to bring a friend?
>   Leslie

Write 20 – 25 words.
Write your note on the answer sheet.

PAPER 2 LISTENING (approximately 25 minutes)

PART 1
QUESTIONS 1 – 5

Listen to the tape.
You will hear five short conversations.
You will hear each conversation twice.
There is one question for each conversation.
For questions 1 – 5, put a tick ✓ under the right answer.

EXAMPLE

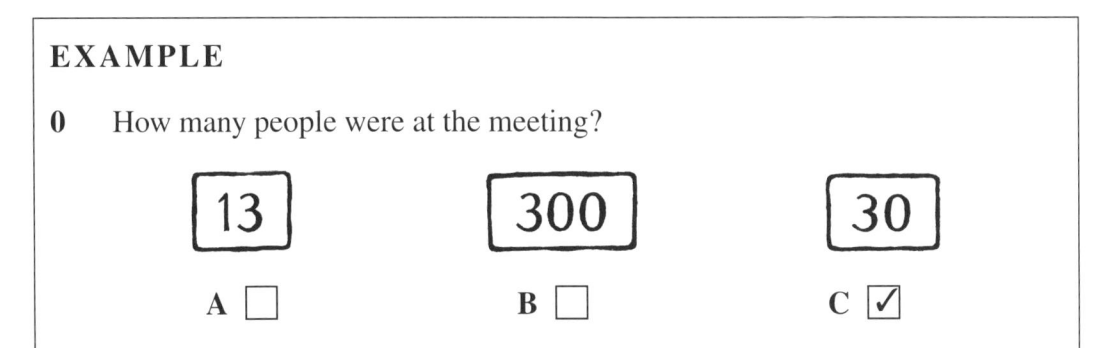

0   How many people were at the meeting?

13	300	30
A ☐	B ☐	C ✓

---

1   What is John going to do tonight?

A ☐   B ☐   C ☐

2   Which is Ben's family?

A ☐   B ☐   C ☐

Test 2

3   Which bag does the woman buy?

A ☐   B ☐   C ☐

4   How much did the woman pay for the apples?

A ☐   B ☐   C ☐

5   What time does the film start?

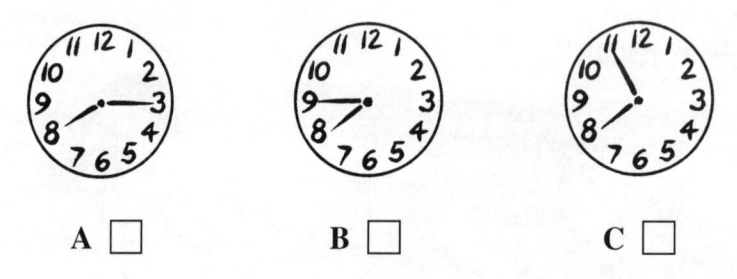

A ☐   B ☐   C ☐

PART 2

QUESTIONS 6 – 10

Listen to Liz and Michael talking about rooms in a hotel.
They are going to paint the rooms.
What colour are they going to paint each room?

For questions 6 – 10, write a letter A – H next to each room.
You will hear the conversation twice.

EXAMPLE		
0	dining room	G

ROOMS   **COLOURS**

6 television room ☐   **A** dark blue

                                B light blue
7 first floor bedrooms ☐
                                C dark green

8 second floor bedrooms ☐ **D** light green

                                E grey
9 office ☐
                                F red

10 kitchen ☐   **G** white

                                H light yellow

Test 2

PART 3
QUESTIONS 11 – 15

Listen to Sarah talking to her friend, Jane, about a new job.

For questions 11 – 15, tick ✓ A, B or C.
You will hear the conversation twice.

EXAMPLE

0 Sarah's boss wants a new

   A   manager. ☐

   B   shop assistant. ☐

   C   secretary. ✓

---

11 Sarah usually starts work at

   A   6.00. ☐

   B   8.30. ☐

   C   9.00. ☐

12 In the new job, Jane can earn

   A   £160 a week. ☐

   B   £180 a week. ☐

   C   £210 a week. ☐

13 Sarah has lunch

   A   in a café. ☐

   B   in a park. ☐

   C   at home. ☐

Paper 2: Listening

14   In the new job, Jane can have

    A   3 weeks' holiday. ☐

    B   4 weeks' holiday. ☐

    C   5 weeks' holiday. ☐

15   The manager's name is Mr

    A   Fawset. ☐

    B   Fawcett. ☐

    C   Fausett. ☐

Test 2

PART 4

QUESTIONS 16 – 20

You will hear a student telephoning a school.

Listen and complete questions 16 – 20.
You will hear the conversation twice.

Notebook

Name of school: **International Language School**

Next course begins

Day: **16** _____

Date: **17** *3rd*

Classes begin at: **18** _____

Address: **19** _____ **London Road**

Near: **20** _____

PART 5

QUESTIONS 21 – 25

You will hear a tour guide talking about a town in Scotland.

Listen and complete questions 21 – 25.
You will hear the information twice.

Notes

Guide's name: Jim

Banks open from: **21** _____

to: **22** _____

closed on: **23** _____

Bus to city centre

number: **24** _____

cost: **25** _____

You now have 8 minutes to write your answers on the answer sheet.

Test 2

PAPER 3 SPEAKING

The Speaking test lasts 8 to 10 minutes. You will take the test with another candidate. There are two examiners, but only one of them will talk to you. The examiner will ask you questions and ask you to talk to the other candidate.

Part 1 (5 – 6 minutes)

The examiner will ask you and your partner some questions. These questions will be about your daily life, past experience and future plans. For example, you may have to speak about your school, job, hobbies or home town.

Part 2 (3 – 4 minutes)

You and your partner will speak to each other. You will ask and answer questions.

Either:

The examiner will give you a card with some words and pictures on it. You will ask your partner five questions using this card. Your partner will answer the questions. Then you will change roles.

Or:

The examiner will give you a card with some information on it. The examiner will give your partner a card with some words on it. Your partner will use the words on the card to ask you questions about the information you have. Then you will change roles.

Test 3

PAPER 1 READING AND WRITING (1 hour 10 minutes)

PART 1
QUESTIONS 1 – 5

Where can you see these notices?
For questions 1 – 5, mark A, B or C on the answer sheet.

EXAMPLE		ANSWER
0 *Return books here*	A in a restaurant B in a bank C in a library	C

1 NO MORE THAN 5 PEOPLE
  A on a bus
  B in a lift
  C in a church

2 HALF PRICE SALE
  A at a station
  B in a theatre
  C in a shop

3 PARKING FOR GUESTS ONLY
  A outside a church
  B outside a hotel
  C outside a zoo

4 COLLECT LUGGAGE HERE
  A in an airport
  B in a café
  C in an office

5 DRY CLEAN ONLY
  A on a window
  B on a coat
  C in a bank

41

Test 3

QUESTIONS 6 – 10

Which notice (A – H) says this (6 – 10)?
For questions 6 – 10, mark the correct letter A – H on the answer sheet.

EXAMPLE	ANSWER
0 You cannot have a cigarette here.	H

6   You can get a car at any time.

7   You pay the same price but you get more.

8   In the evening, children may not come in.

9   There are two prices for tickets.

10   You can buy food here on Sunday.

A   TOMATO JUICE 10% extra - FREE

B   NO RIGHT TURN

C   Admission: £6.00
    Schoolchildren, Students and Over-65s: £3.00

D   Pat's Pizza Place
    Open 12 noon till late, seven days a week.

E   Beach Umbrellas For Hire

F   YELLOWBIRD TAXIS 24-hour service

G   7.30 p.m. – 9.30 p.m. Adult Swimming Only

H   NO SMOKING SECTION

Paper 1: Reading and Writing

PART 2

QUESTIONS 11 – 15

Read the descriptions (11 – 15) of things you can see at the beach.
What is the name of each thing (A – H)?
For questions 11 – 15, mark the correct letter A – H on the answer sheet.

EXAMPLE	ANSWER
0 You lie on this on the beach.	H

11   You eat this when you are hot.

12   You may see these swimming in the water.

13   You play with this on the beach.

14   You may see these on the water.

15   You wear these when it is sunny.

A   ball

B   boats

C   fish

D   ice-cream

E   sea

F   sunglasses

G   suntan cream

H   towel

43

PART 3

QUESTIONS 16 – 20

Complete the five conversations.
For questions 16 – 20, mark A, B or C on the answer sheet.

EXAMPLE		ANSWER
What's the time?	A Tuesday. B Half past eight. C 1998.	B

16 Why don't you ask Sandra?
    A I hope so.
    B Never mind.
    C That's a good idea.

17 Congratulations!
    A I'm sorry.
    B Thank you.
    C What a pity!

18 How is your son?
    A Fine, thanks.
    B Four months old.
    C With his father.

19 Can I help you?
    A At two o'clock.
    B I can help you.
    C Yes, please.

20 I'd like to try those shoes on, please.
    A What size are you?
    B Are they black?
    C Do you like it?

QUESTIONS 21 – 25

Complete the telephone conversation.
What does Tom say to Maria?
For questions 21 – 25, mark the correct letter A – H on the answer sheet.

EXAMPLE	ANSWER
Maria: Hello, Tom. This is Maria.	
Tom: **0**	E

Maria: Fine. Thank you for the party last night. I had a great time.

Tom: **21** ....

Maria: Tom, did I leave my coat at your house last night?

Tom: **22** ....

Maria: It's green with a black collar.

Tom: **23** ....

Maria: I'm going to work now. Can I come and get it this evening?

Tom: **24** ....

Maria: I'll come at 6.30.

Tom: **25** ....

Maria: OK. Goodbye.

A Well, two people left their coats behind. What colour is yours?

B You'll have to come before 7.15. I'm going out then.

C Yes, there's a green one here.

D What time is it?

E Hi Maria, how are you?

F All right, see you later.

G It's a beautiful coat, isn't it?

H Good. I'm glad you enjoyed it.

PART 4

QUESTIONS 26 – 32

Read the article about the Edinburgh Festival.
Are sentences 26 – 32 'Right' (A) or 'Wrong' (B)?

If there is not enough information to answer 'Right' (A) or 'Wrong' (B), choose 'Doesn't say' (C).

For questions 26 – 32, mark A, B, or C on the answer sheet.

Visit the Edinburgh Festival!

Every year, thousands of people come to Edinburgh, the capital city of Scotland, to be part of the Edinburgh Festival. For three weeks every August and September the city is filled with actors and artists from all over the world. They come to Edinburgh for the biggest arts festival in Britain. During this time, the streets of the city are alive with music and dance from early in the morning until late at night. You can even see artists painting pictures on the streets!

Tens of thousands of tourists come to the Festival to see new films and plays and to hear music played by famous musicians. This year, you can see over five hundred performances with actors from more than forty countries.

The tickets for these performances are quite cheap, and it is usually easier to see your favourite star in Edinburgh than it is in London. So come to Edinburgh next summer!

EXAMPLE	ANSWER
0 Edinburgh is the capital of Scotland. **A** Right **B** Wrong **C** Doesn't say	A

26   The Edinburgh Festival is a month long.

     A Right   **B** Wrong   **C** Doesn't say

27   The Edinburgh Festival is in October.

     A Right   **B** Wrong   **C** Doesn't say

28   Actors come to the Edinburgh Festival from lots of different countries.

     A Right   **B** Wrong   **C** Doesn't say

29   You can hear music all day.

     A Right   **B** Wrong   **C** Doesn't say

30   More than ten thousand students come to the Edinburgh Festival every year.

     A Right   **B** Wrong   **C** Doesn't say

31   It is expensive to go the theatre in Edinburgh.

     A Right   **B** Wrong   **C** Doesn't say

32   It is usually more difficult to see famous actors in London than in Edinburgh.

     A Right   **B** Wrong   **C** Doesn't say

Test 3

PART 5

QUESTION 33 – 40

Read the information about rhinos.
Choose the best word (A, B or C) for each space (33 – 40).
For questions 33 – 40, mark A, B or C on the answer sheet.

THE RHINO

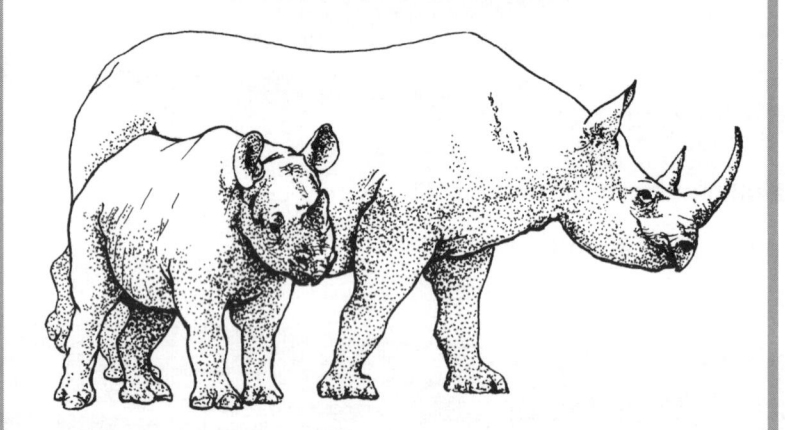

There __0__ five different types of rhino in the world today. The Black and White Rhino live in __33__ open fields of Africa. The others live in forests in Asia.

All rhinos have big, heavy bodies. Their skin is very hard and they have very __34__ hair. The great body __35__ the rhino stands __36__ four short legs. Each foot has three toes. They usually walk very __37__, but they can run at 50 kilometres an hour. Rhinos are usually quiet and calm animals, and they only __38__ grass and other plants.

A baby rhino weighs 40 kilos when it is born. It has been inside its mother __39__ about fifteen months. An adult rhino weighs over 200 kilos and may __40__ to be 50 years old.

Paper 1: Reading and Writing

EXAMPLE						ANSWER
0	**A** are	**B**	is	**C**	were	A

33	**A**	these	**B**	the	**C**	an
34	**A**	little	**B**	many	**C**	few
35	**A**	to	**B**	of	**C**	for
36	**A**	on	**B**	in	**C**	at
37	**A**	slow	**B**	slower	**C**	slowly
38	**A**	eat	**B**	eats	**C**	ate
39	**A**	since	**B**	during	**C**	for
40	**A**	lives	**B**	living	**C**	live

PART 6

QUESTIONS 41 – 50

Complete this letter.
Write ONE word for each space (41 – 50).
For questions 41 – 50, write your words on the answer sheet.

---

17 Green Street
Camden
London

9 August 1997

Dear John,

Thank you for helping (*Example:* __me__) with my English. You are __41__ very good teacher. I enjoyed my stay __42__ Cambridge.

Now I am staying at my brother's flat. __43__ is studying to be a doctor. I will stay __44__ him for two weeks and then go home __45__ Greece.

I like London very __46__ . We __47__ to Regent's Park by bus yesterday. It __48__ very sunny and we had a good time.

Tonight, I am __49__ to see a film with my brother and some __50__ his friends.

I'll write again from Greece.

Best wishes,
    Kostas

PART 7

QUESTIONS 51 – 55

Read this information about a girl who wants to go to a summer camp for young people.
Fill in the information on the Application Form.
For questions 51 – 55, write the information on the answer sheet.

> Claire is in the 9th year at school. She lives at Crow Cottage, Bradley with her parents, Linda and Derek Drake. She is 13 years old and likes swimming and playing the piano. She is going to camp with her best friend, Rosie Brown.

YOUNG PEOPLE'S CAMP

Application Form

First name:	*Claire*
Surname:	**51**
Age next birthday:	**52**
Address:	**53**
Hobbies:	**54**
I would like to be in the same tent as:	**55**

Test 3

PART 8
QUESTION 56

Read the note from your friend, Eric.
Write a note to answer his questions.

> I'll make the meal tonight.
> Would you like meat or fish?
> What vegetables do you want?
> What time will you be home?
>
> Best wishes
>
> Eric

Write 20 – 25 words.
Write your note on the answer sheet.

PAPER 2 LISTENING (approximately 25 minutes)

PART 1
QUESTIONS 1 – 5

Listen to the tape.
You will hear five short conversations.
You will hear each conversation twice.
There is one question for each conversation.
For questions 1 – 5, put a tick ✓ under the right answer.

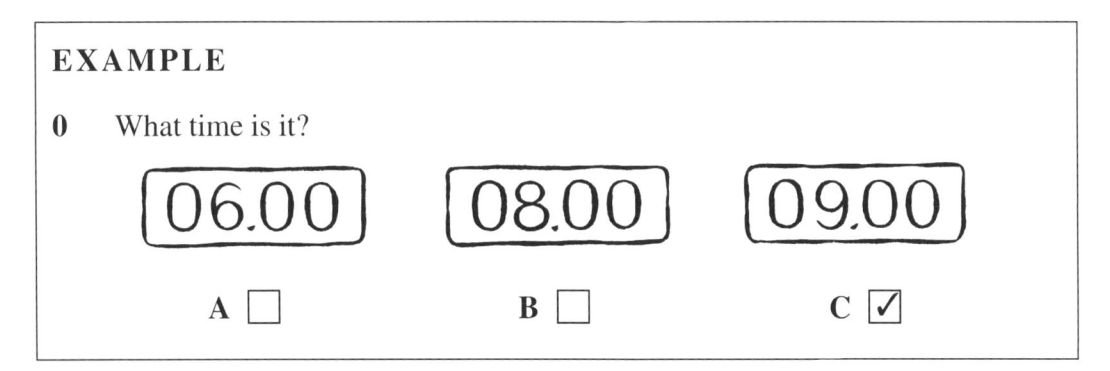

EXAMPLE

0   What time is it?

06.00	08.00	09.00
A ☐	B ☐	C ✓

1   How does the man travel to Liverpool?

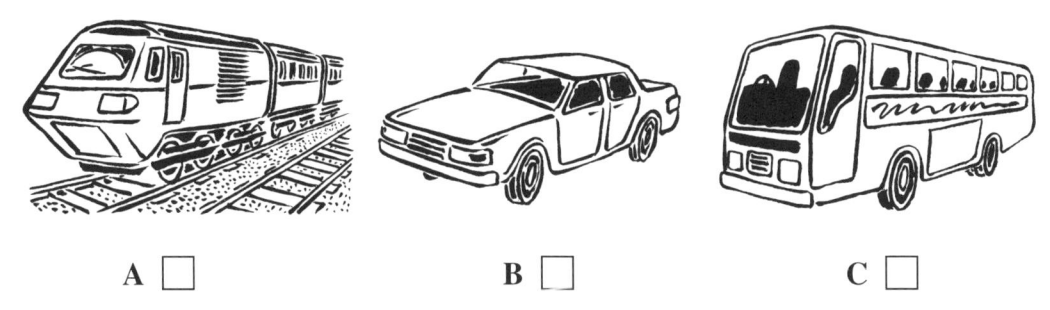

A ☐   B ☐   C ☐

2   Which bill has just arrived?

GAS   WATER   ELECTRICITY

A ☐   B ☐   C ☐

53

Test 3

3 What will they do tomorrow afternoon?

A ☐ B ☐ C ☐

4 How did the man hear about the fire?

A ☐ B ☐ C ☐

5 What time did Mr Thompson ring?

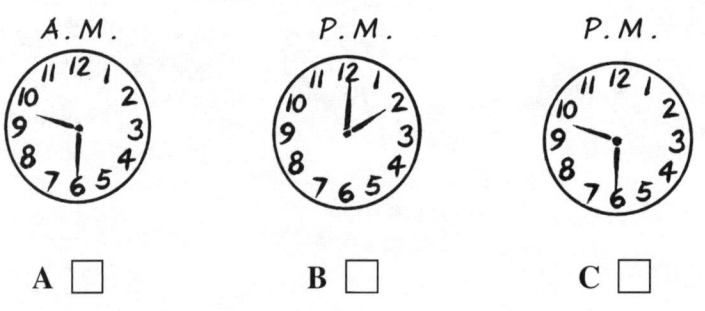

A ☐ B ☐ C ☐

PART 2

QUESTIONS 6 – 10

Listen to two people talking at a party.
What do the guests want to eat or drink?

For questions 6 – 10, write a letter A – H next to each person.
You will hear the conversation twice.

EXAMPLE		
0	Kevin	E

PEOPLE

6 Barbara ☐

7 Paul ☐

8 Diana ☐

9 Jim ☐

10 Julie ☐

FOOD AND DRINK

A coffee

B coke

C ice-cream

D milk

E orange juice

F sandwich

G tea

H water

PART 3

QUESTIONS 11 – 15

Listen to a conversation in a travel agency.

For questions 11 – 15, tick ✓ A, B or C.
You will hear the conversation twice.

EXAMPLE

0 You can fly to Buenos Aires

    A once a week. ☐

    B twice a week. ☐

    C three times a week. ✓

---

11 The plane leaves at

    A 12 a.m. ☐

    B 2 p.m. ☐

    C 3 p.m. ☐

12 The bus station is in

    A Bill Street. ☐

    B Hill Street. ☐

    C Mill Street. ☐

13 The journey to the airport takes

    A 1 hour 15 minutes. ☐

    B 1 hour 30 minutes. ☐

    C 1 hour 45 minutes. ☐

Paper 2: Listening

14 The man's ticket to Buenos Aires will cost

    A £240. ☐

    B £300. ☐

    C £320. ☐

15 The coach costs

    A £13.50. ☐

    B £14.50. ☐

    C £30.50. ☐

Test 3

PART 4

QUESTIONS 16 – 20

You will hear a conversation about Toni.

Listen and complete questions 16 – 20.
You will hear the conversation twice.

Toni's had an accident.

He's hurt his:	leg
Name of hospital:	**16**
Room:	**17**
Floor:	**18**
Visiting hours:	**19** 4 p.m to .... every afternoon
Please take:	**20**

Paper 2: Listening

PART 5

QUESTIONS 21 – 25

You will hear some information about a farm.

Listen and complete questions 21 – 25.
You will hear the information twice.

PARK FARM

To see:	Farm Animals	
Food in:	**21** _____	Cat Tea Room
Opens at:	**22** _____	
Closes at:	5 p.m.	
Family ticket costs:	**23** £ _____	
Don't bring:	**24** _____	
Not far from:	**25** _____	

You now have 8 minutes to write your answers on the answer sheet.

Test 3

PAPER 3   SPEAKING

The Speaking test lasts 8 to 10 minutes. You will take the test with another candidate. There are two examiners, but only one of them will talk to you. The examiner will ask you questions and ask you to talk to the other candidate.

Part 1 (5 – 6 minutes)

The examiner will ask you and your partner some questions. These questions will be about your daily life, past experience and future plans. For example, you may have to speak about your school, job, hobbies or home town.

Part 2 (3 – 4 minutes)

You and your partner will speak to each other. You will ask and answer questions.

Either:

The examiner will give you a card with some words and pictures on it. You will ask your partner five questions using this card. Your partner will answer the questions. Then you will change roles.

Or:

The examiner will give you a card with some information on it. The examiner will give your partner a card with some words on it. Your partner will use the words on the card to ask you questions about the information you have. Then you will change roles.

Test 4

PAPER 1 READING AND WRITING (1 hour 10 minutes)

PART 1
QUESTIONS 1 – 5

Where can you see these notices?
For questions 1 – 5, mark A, B or C on the answer sheet.

EXAMPLE		ANSWER
0 One Way Traffic →	A in a school B in an office C on a road	C

1 Book your train tickets here.
   A at a railway station
   B in a theatre
   C at a bus stop

2 *Fresh bread* DAILY
   A in a bank
   B in a shop
   C in a theatre

3 LAST PETROL STATION FOR 50 MILES
   A on a motorway
   B in a railway station
   C at an airport

4 ◄ Emergencies   Appointments ►
   A in a zoo
   B in a hospital
   C in a hotel

5 *For pain:* take two tablets
   A on a medicine bottle
   B on a food packet
   C on a soap box

Test 4

QUESTIONS 6 – 10

Which notice (A – H) says this (6 – 10)?
For questions 6 – 10, mark the correct letter A – H on the answer sheet.

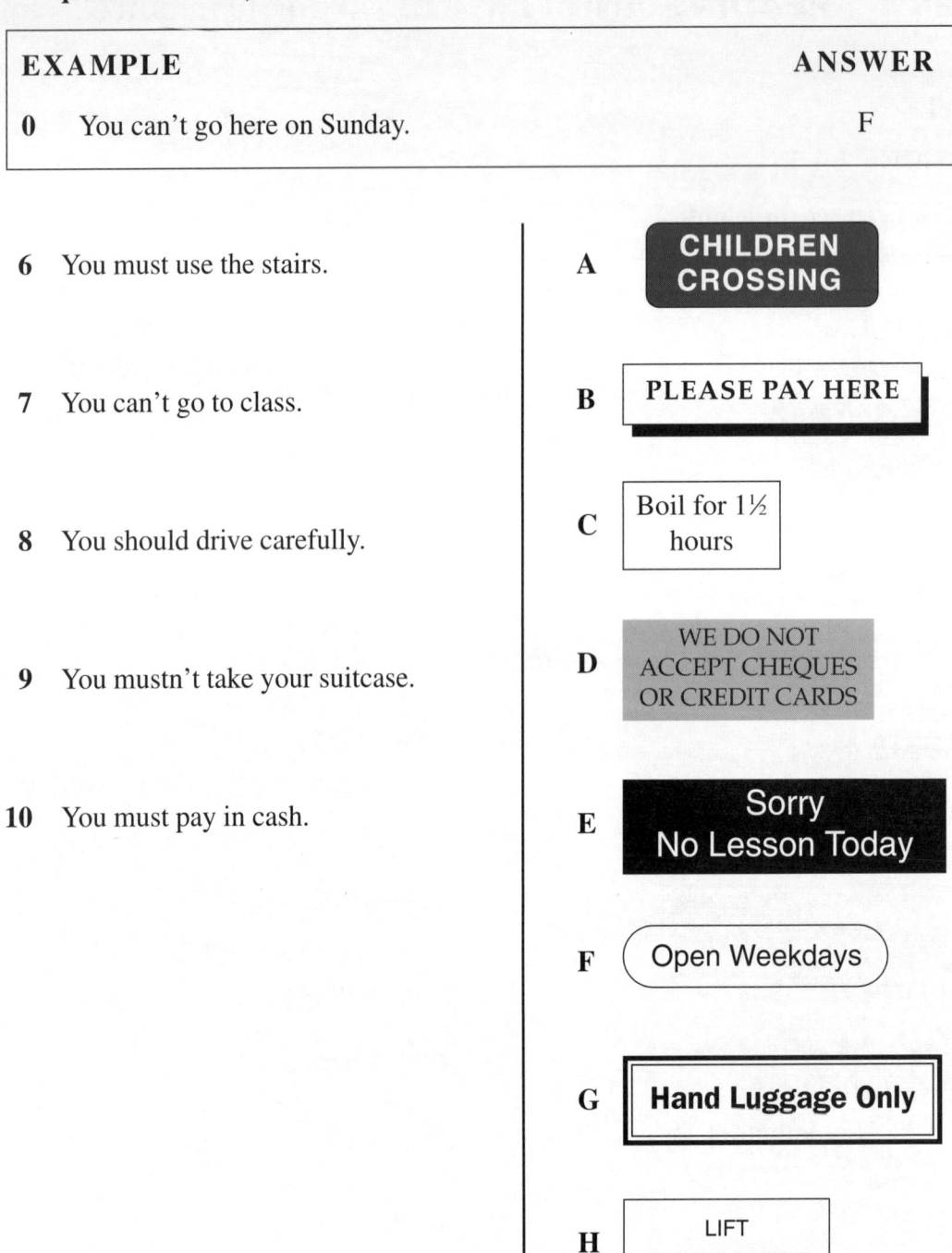

EXAMPLE	ANSWER
0 You can't go here on Sunday.	F

6   You must use the stairs.

7   You can't go to class.

8   You should drive carefully.

9   You mustn't take your suitcase.

10   You must pay in cash.

A   CHILDREN CROSSING

B   PLEASE PAY HERE

C   Boil for 1½ hours

D   WE DO NOT ACCEPT CHEQUES OR CREDIT CARDS

E   Sorry No Lesson Today

F   Open Weekdays

G   Hand Luggage Only

H   LIFT OUT OF ORDER

PART 2

QUESTIONS 11 – 15

**Read the descriptions (11 – 15) of some parts of the body.
What is the name of each part of the body (A – H)?
For questions 11 – 15, mark the correct letter A – H on the answer sheet.**

EXAMPLE	ANSWER
0 This grows on your head.	D

PARTS OF THE BODY

11 You have got five of these on each foot.

A   ears

B   eyes

12 You hear with these.

C   fingers

D   hair

13 You use these when you walk.

E   legs

F   teeth

14 You see with these.

G   toes

15 You have got this in your mouth.

H   tongue

PART 3

QUESTIONS 16 – 20

Complete the five conversations.
For questions 16 – 20, mark A, B or C on the answer sheet.

EXAMPLE

What's the time?

A Tuesday.
B Half past eight.
C 1998.

ANSWER

B

16 Excuse me, when does the next train leave?

A From Platform 4.
B Yesterday.
C In ten minutes.

17 When can we go to the cinema?

A I'm free on Saturday.
B I like the cinema.
C I hope you can come.

18 Have a good holiday.

A You have.
B You will.
C You too.

19 How do you like your meat done?

A I don't like it.
B I like it very much.
C I like it well done.

20 How do you do?

A Very well.
B I'm a doctor.
C How do you do?

QUESTIONS 21 – 25

Complete the conversation.
What does David say to the waiter?
For questions 21 – 25, mark the correct letter A – H on the answer sheet.

EXAMPLE	ANSWER
Waiter: Good evening, sir. How can I help you?	
David: **0**	B

Waiter: Certainly, sir. This one by the window?

David: **21** ....

Waiter: And what would you like to eat?

David: **22** ....

Waiter: Spaghetti with meat and tomato sauce is very nice, or there is four-cheese pizza.

David: **23** ....

Waiter: Fine. And would you like anything with it? Garlic bread or ...

David: **24** ....

Waiter: OK. And to drink?

David: **25** ....

Waiter: Yes, certainly. So that's one four-cheese pizza, one green salad and one mineral water. Thank you, sir.

A Have you got mineral water?

B Good evening. I'd like a table for one.

C How much is it?

D What have you got?

E I think I'll have the pizza.

F Can you bring me the menu, please?

G Nothing more, thanks. Oh yes, perhaps a green salad.

H Yes, that's fine.

PART 4
QUESTIONS 26 – 32

Read the article about burglars.
Are sentences 26 – 32 'Right' (A) or 'Wrong' (B)?

If there is not enough information to answer 'Right' (A) or 'Wrong' (B), choose 'Doesn't say' (C).

For questions 26 – 32, mark A, B or C on the answer sheet.

BURGLARS LOVE THE AFTERNOON

MOST house burglaries happen between 2 p.m. and 6 p.m., say the police.

Inspector Ian Saunders told our newspaper that the number of house burglaries has gone up by more than 30% compared with last year. He also said that 67% of burglaries happen when people have gone out and left a door or window open.

He went on to report that night-time burglaries are unusual because families are usually at home at that time. But he said that winter afternoons are the best time for burglars because it is dark and they can't be seen easily. Also many houses are empty at that time.

Inspector Saunders said that it is a good idea to leave lights on in living rooms and bedrooms to keep burglars away. He also asked neighbours to watch the other houses in the street when people are away. They should call the police if they see anything strange. 'We will also tell you how to make your house safe,' Inspector Saunders said. 'This kind of help costs nothing.'

Paper 1: Reading and Writing

EXAMPLE			**ANSWER**
0	Most burglaries happen in the morning.		B
	A Right **B** Wrong **C** Doesn't say		

26 The number of house burglaries is the same as last year.
A Right   **B** Wrong   **C** Doesn't say

27 Most burglars are men.
A Right   **B** Wrong   **C** Doesn't say

28 People sometimes make things easy for burglars.
A Right   **B** Wrong   **C** Doesn't say

29 The summer is more difficult for burglars.
A Right   **B** Wrong   **C** Doesn't say

30 Burglars don't usually go to houses with lights on.
A Right   **B** Wrong   **C** Doesn't say

31 Burglars usually drive cars.
A Right   **B** Wrong   **C** Doesn't say

32 You have to pay for information from the police.
A Right   **B** Wrong   **C** Doesn't say

PART 5

QUESTIONS 33 – 40

Read the information about Madame Tussaud's museum in London.
Choose the best word (A, B or C) for each space (33 – 40).
For questions 33 – 40, mark A, B or C on the answer sheet.

Madame Tussaud's

One very famous place for tourists in London is Madame Tussaud's museum. Here people __0__ see figures of famous people made of wax.

Madame Tussaud was born __33__ France in 1761. Her uncle, a doctor, __34__ wax figures of people. He opened __35__ museum of these figures in Paris. Marie helped __36__ in his work.

In 1789, during the French Revolution, Marie __37__ sent to prison. Here she had to copy __38__ heads of famous people when they were dead, including Queen Marie Antoinette's.

In 1795, Marie married François Tussaud __39__ in 1802 she came to London with her wax figures. Here she opened a museum and her figures can __40__ be seen today.

EXAMPLE						ANSWER
0	A can	B	must	C	shall	A

33	A	at	B	by	C	in
34	A	make	B	made	C	makes
35	A	a	B	one	C	some
36	A	her	B	him	C	them
37	A	has	B	is	C	was
38	A	any	B	the	C	those
39	A	and	B	because	C	when
40	A	ever	B	still	C	yet

PART 6
QUESTIONS 41 – 50

Complete the memos.
Write ONE word for each space (41 – 50).
For questions 41 – 50, write your words on the answer sheet.

Memo

To:	All staff	From: D Brown
Subject:	Holidays	Date: 22.2.97

I (*Example:* am) planning the holidays for next year. Please __41__ me when you would like __42__ take your holiday. If possible, __43__ you give me two dates? Please give me __44__ answer by the end __45__ the month.

Thank you.

D Brown

Memo

To:	D Brown	From: J Green
Subject:	Holidays	Date: 23.2.97

Could I take two weeks' holiday __46__ July? I'd __47__ to take the first two weeks, but if __48__ is not possible, the last two weeks will __49__ OK. Also, can __50__ take three extra days in the first week of December?

John

PART 7

QUESTIONS 51 – 55

Read the information about Jane Forrest. She wants a university student to stay in her house.
Fill in the information on the Application Form.
For questions 51 – 55, write the information on the answer sheet.

> Jane Forrest lives at 3 Bridge Avenue, Newcastle. She is a teacher. She has a large house with four bedrooms and two bathrooms. The house is eight miles from the university. She can give students breakfast and supper but not lunch.

Application Form (Student Guest)

First name:	*Jane*
Surname:	**51**
Job:	**52**
Address:	**53**
Type of house:	*Large – 4 bedrooms*
How far from university?	**54**
Number of meals per day:	**55**

Test 4

PART 8
QUESTION 56

You cannot be at the railway station when your father arrives there. Your friend is going to meet him for you.

Write a note to your friend.

Say:

- **when** your father will arrive.
- **what** he looks like.

Write 20 – 25 words.
Write your note on the answer sheet.

PAPER 2   LISTENING (approximately 25 minutes)

PART 1

QUESTIONS 1 – 5

Listen to the tape.
You will hear five short conversations.
You will hear each conversation twice.
There is one question for each conversation.
For questions 1 – 5, put a tick ✓ under the right answer.

EXAMPLE

0   How many people were at the meeting?

13	300	30
A ☐	B ☐	C ✓

---

1   When is the party?

Tuesday	Wednesday	Thursday
A ☐	B ☐	C ☐

2   Where are the glasses?

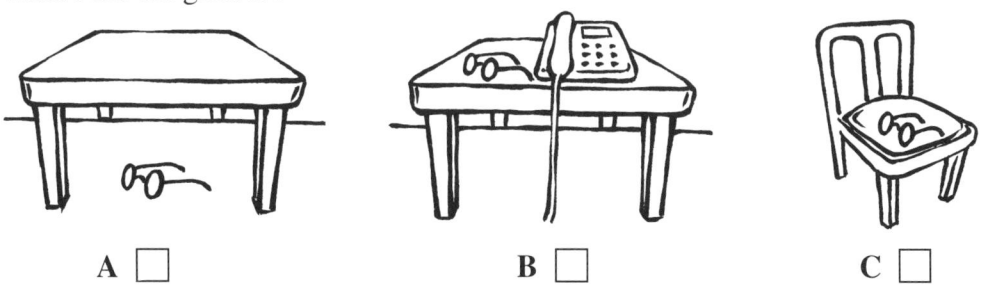

| A ☐ | B ☐ | C ☐ |

73

Test 4

3   How much are the shoes?

A ☐   B ☐   C ☐

4   What will the weather be like in the afternoon?

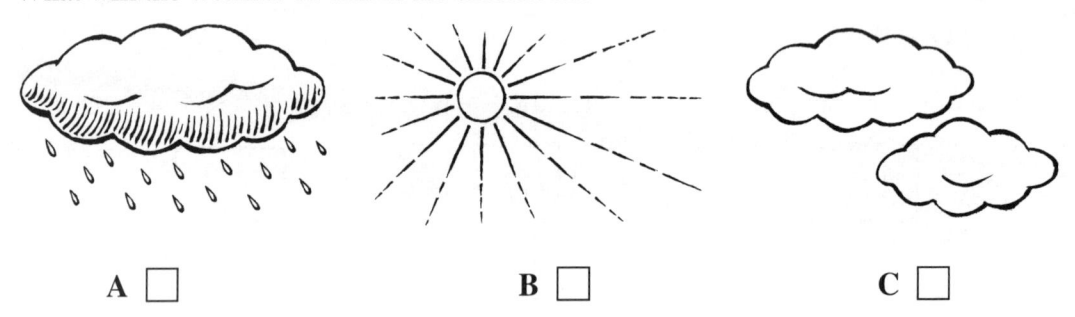

A ☐   B ☐   C ☐

5   What time will she take the train?

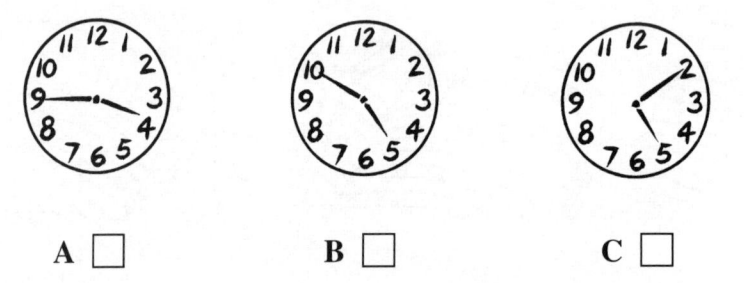

A ☐   B ☐   C ☐

74

PART 2

QUESTIONS 6 – 10

Listen to Teresa talking to Paul about presents for his family. What is she going to buy for each person?

For questions 6 – 10, write a letter A – H next to each person. You will hear the conversation twice.

EXAMPLE		
0	Kevin	A

PEOPLE

6   Jon   ☐

7   Ann   ☐

8   Mother   ☐

9   Father   ☐

10 Paul   ☐

PRESENTS

A   book

B   cassette

C   football

D   meal

E   shirt

F   theatre tickets

G   tie

H   video

Test 4

PART 3

QUESTIONS 11 – 15

Listen to Carlos making a phone call.

For questions 11 – 15, tick ✓ A, B or C.
You will hear the conversation twice.

EXAMPLE

0 The library is closed until

A	Tuesday.	☐
B	Wednesday.	☐
C	Thursday.	✓

---

11 What must Carlos take to the library?

A	a student card	☐
B	a teacher's letter	☐
C	a passport	☐

12 How much will it cost Carlos to join?

A	1,500 pesetas	☐
B	3,000 pesetas	☐
C	4,000 pesetas	☐

13 Carlos will get

A	2 library tickets.	☐
B	3 library tickets.	☐
C	4 library tickets.	☐

Paper 2: Listening

14   On Saturdays, the library opens at

   A   10.30. ☐

   B   11.00. ☐

   C   2.30. ☐

15   The library is in

   A   Murdoch Street. ☐

   B   Murdosh Street. ☐

   C   Murdock Street. ☐

Test 4

PART 4

QUESTIONS 16 – 20

You will hear a woman telephoning a garage about her car.

Listen and complete questions 16 – 20.
You will hear the conversation twice.

Jackson's Garage

Customer's name:		Mary Wilson
Trouble with car:	16	
Office address:	17	31 .... Road
Customer's phone number:	18	
Time of appointment:	19	
Colour of car:	20	

Paper 2: Listening

PART 5

QUESTIONS 21 – 25

You will hear a man talking on the radio.

Listen and complete questions 21 – 25.
You will hear the information twice.

Old School Friends

Please contact

First name:		Janet
Last name:	**21**	
Name of school:	**22**	Green .... School
From:	**23**	
To:	**24**	
Telephone number:	**25**	

You now have 8 minutes to write your answers on the answer sheet.

Test 4

PAPER 3 SPEAKING

The Speaking test lasts 8 to 10 minutes. You will take the test with another candidate. There are two examiners, but only one of them will talk to you. The examiner will ask you questions and ask you to talk to the other candidate.

Part 1 (5 – 6 minutes)

The examiner will ask you and your partner some questions. These questions will be about your daily life, past experience and future plans. For example, you may have to speak about your school, job, hobbies or home town.

Part 2 (3 – 4 minutes)

You and your partner will speak to each other. You will ask and answer questions.

Either:

The examiner will give you a card with some words and pictures on it. You will ask your partner five questions using this card. Your partner will answer the questions. Then you will change roles.

Or:

The examiner will give you a card with some information on it. The examiner will give your partner a card with some words on it. Your partner will use the words on the card to ask you questions about the information you have. Then you will change roles.

Visual materials for Paper 3

1A

FOOD

Ask your partner questions about food.

Breakfast?

Like best?

Cook?

How often?

Drink?

Visual materials

2D

THE PRESENT

- who for?

- why?

- name of book?

- price? £ ?

- shop?

4A

SCHOOL TRIP TO LONDON

Saturday 24th April

Morning   -   Buckingham Palace
Lunch   -   1.00 p.m.
Afternoon -   shopping

TAKE YOUR RAINCOAT !!

HOME

Ask your partner about his/her home.

Address?

House/Flat?

Rooms? | 2 | | 4 | | ? |

Near?

Who with?

2C

TO: David
Happy Birthday!

ENGLISH MADE EASY

WHITE'S BOOKSHOP

ENGLISH
MADE
EASY   £4.99

TOTAL   £4.99

Thank you

3A

North London Language School

BUSINESS ENGLISH COURSE
Starts April 29

4-week course
15 hours every week

£180

2B

PARTY

- where?

- whose party?

- why?

- finish? 🕐 ?

- dance?

4C

SWIMMING POOL

Times: Mon-Sat   7.30 am - 8.00 pm
            Sun   8.00 am - 6.30 pm

Tickets: Adult   £1.75
            Under-16s   70p

Swimming Lessons for Children: Saturday morning

Cafe: open every day

ORFORD SPORTS CENTRE, NORMAN ROAD

BOOKSHOP

- name of bookshop?

- English dictionaries?

- closing time?

- open Saturday?

- address?

SWIMMING POOL

- ♦ **opening times?**

- ♦ **price? £ ?**

- ♦ **address?**

- ♦ **cafe?**

- ♦ **lessons for children?**

2A

COME TO PETER'S PARTY

HE'S PASSED HIS EXAMS !!

GRAND HOTEL

SATURDAY NIGHT

8 - 11.30

LIVE MUSIC !

DISCO !

3C

New England Bookshop
18 Preston Road

BOOKS FOR LANGUAGE LEARNING
DICTIONARIES
TRAVEL BOOKS

Monday - Friday
9am - 8pm

3B

LANGUAGE SCHOOL

- name of school?

- English classes?

- number of hours?

- price?   £ ?

- begin?

4B

SCHOOL TRIP

- where to?

- day?

- visit?

- take anything?

- lunch? 🕐 ?

Sample answer sheet – Reading and Writing (Sheet 1)

CAMBRIDGE
EXAMINATIONS, CERTIFICATES & DIPLOMAS
ENGLISH AS A FOREIGN LANGUAGE

University of Cambridge
Local Examinations Syndicate
International Examinations

FOR SUPERVISOR'S USE ONLY
Shade here if the candidate is ABSENT or has WITHDRAWN

Examination Details

Examination Title

Centre/Candidate No.

Candidate Name

- Sign here if the details above are correct.

- Tell the Supervisor now if the details above are not correct.

KET Reading and Writing Answer Sheet

Use a pencil Mark ONE letter for each question.

For example:

If you think C is the right answer to the question, mark your answer sheet like this:

Change your answer like this:

Part 1
1. A B C
2. A B C
3. A B C
4. A B C
5. A B C
6. A B C D E F G H
7. A B C D E F G H
8. A B C D E F G H
9. A B C D E F G H
10. A B C D E F G H

Part 2
11. A B C D E F G H
12. A B C D E F G H
13. A B C D E F G H
14. A B C D E F G H
15. A B C D E F G H

Part 3
16. A B C
17. A B C
18. A B C
19. A B C
20. A B C
21. A B C D E F G H
22. A B C D E F G H
23. A B C D E F G H
24. A B C D E F G H
25. A B C D E F G H

Part 4
26. A B C
27. A B C
28. A B C
29. A B C
30. A B C
31. A B C
32. A B C

Part 5
33. A B C
34. A B C
35. A B C
36. A B C
37. A B C
38. A B C
39. A B C
40. A B C

Turn over for Parts 6 - 8 →

© UCLES/K&J *You may photocopy this page.*

Sample answer sheet – Reading and Writing (Sheet 2)

Use a pencil

For Parts 6 and 7, write your answers in the spaces next to the numbers (41 to 55) like this:

| 0 | *example* | 0 |

	Part 6	Do not write here
41		41
42		42
43		43
44		44
45		45
46		46
47		47
48		48
49		49
50		50

	Part 7	Do not write here
51		51
52		52
53		53
54		54
55		55

Part 8 (Question 56): Write your answer here

Do not write below (Examiner use only)

0   1   2   3   4   5

© UCLES/K&J *You may photocopy this page.*

Sample answer sheet – Listening

CAMBRIDGE EXAMINATIONS, CERTIFICATES & DIPLOMAS — ENGLISH AS A FOREIGN LANGUAGE

University of Cambridge Local Examinations Syndicate International Examinations

FOR SUPERVISOR'S USE ONLY
Shade here if the candidate is ABSENT or has WITHDRAWN

Examination Details

Examination Title

Centre/Candidate No.

Candidate Name

- Sign here if the details above are correct.

- Tell the Supervisor now if the details above are not correct.

KET Listening Answer Sheet

Use a pencil

For Parts 1, 2 and 3: Mark ONE letter for each question.

For example, if you think C is the right answer to the question, mark your answer sheet like this: 0 A B C

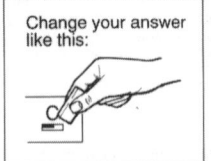

Change your answer like this:

Part 1
1. A B C
2. A B C
3. A B C
4. A B C
5. A B C

Part 2
6. A B C D E F G H
7. A B C D E F G H
8. A B C D E F G H
9. A B C D E F G H
10. A B C D E F G H

Part 3
11. A B C
12. A B C
13. A B C
14. A B C
15. A B C

For Parts 4 and 5: Write your answers in the spaces next to the numbers (16 - 25) like this: 0 *example*

Part 4
		Do not write here
16		16
17		17
18		18
19		19
20		20

Part 5
		Do not write here
21		21
22		22
23		23
24		24
25		25

© UCLES/K&J *You may photocopy this page.*